Dear Parent,

Moving from being a nonreader to a reader is one of the most magical transitions in life. For some children, it happens with lightning speed. For others, more slowly. Whatever your child's experience may be, the best way to encourage reading ability is to focus on the enjoyment and fun of a story.

Here are some ways to support success:

In the beginning, read the story aloud a few times, with the child at your side. Be sure to read in character, to bring the words to life.

Run your finger under the text as you read to help the child connect printed and spoken words. Before you know it, he or she will be participating in the reading.

Let the child fill in words as you read through the book, especially predictable or repeated phrases or words that complete rhymes.

If the child tries to sound out words, encourage the activity—but never force a child to struggle unduly with a word. Just say the word, let him or her repeat it, and move on.

As you read, allow your child to linger on a page as long as he or she likes, examining the pictures or discussing the story with you.

First and foremost, share in the fun and excitement of the story. Realizing that reading is fun is your child's first step toward becoming a reader!

For Matthew—
J.N.

For Tony and Mayme—
Two loving people that gave me my first bear,
taught me to count, and much, much more.
D.S.

Parents
MAGAZINE
P L A Y ■ L E A R N

Learning
Horizons®

AN AMERICAN GREETINGS COMPANY

A+ Readers

Level 1+

Counting BEARS

by Judy Nayer
Illustrated by Dom Scibilia

One bear by himself.

Two bears on the shelf.

But where's my bear?

6

Three bears on the floor.

Four bears
by the door.

But where's my bear?

Five bears on the stair.

Six bears in the chair.

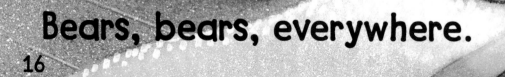

Bears, bears, everywhere.

But where's my bear?

18 Seven bears in a row.

Eight bears
high and low.

Bears, bears, everywhere.

But where's my bear?

Nine bears in the grass.

Ten bears let me pass.

And then—at last!
What do I see?

One bear in a heap.
It's **MY** bear!

Now I can sleep.